Hide-and-Seek Visual Adventures

UNCOVER HISTORY

Published in 2010 by Windmill Books, LLC
303 Park Avenue South, Suite 1280
New York, NY 10010-3657

First published in 2009 by Orpheus Books Ltd.,
6 Church Green, Witney, Oxfordshire, OX28 4AW

Created and produced by Nicholas Harris, Sarah Hartley, Erica Williams, and Katie Sexton
Orpheus Books Ltd.

Illustrated by Peter Kent

Text by Olivia Brookes

Library of Congress Cataloging-in-Publication Data

Brookes, Olivia.
Uncover history / [text by Olivia Brooks] ; illustrated by Peter Kent.
    p. cm. -- (Hide-and-seek visual adventures)
Includes bibliographical references and index.
ISBN 978-1-60754-653-5 (library binding : alk. paper)
1. World history--Pictorial works--Juvenile literature. 2. World history--Juvenile literature. I. Peter
Kent. II. Title.

D21.1.B76 2010
909--dc22
                              2009032822

Printed and bound in China

CPSIA compliance information: Batch # OR9002019: For further information contact Windmill Books, New York, New York at 1-866-478-0556.

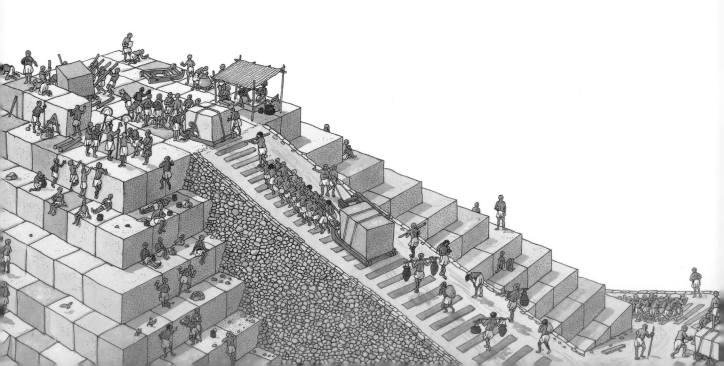

Hide-and-Seek Visual Adventures

UNCOVER
HISTORY

Illustrated by Peter Kent

an imprint of
WINDMILL BOOKS
New York

Contents

Introduction

This book takes you on an exciting journey into the past. You can find out what it was like to live in the days of Ancient Egypt or Rome. You can have fun exploring a castle or a galleon in their days of glory, ride in a stagecoach in the Wild West, or join the *Titanic* on its fateful voyage. The illustrator has taken the walls off some of the buildings and ships to let you take a look inside. You can see the Roman baths, the Great Hall of a castle, the lower decks of a galleon, and many other fascinating places. Check out the index for a list of all the the things there are to discover in this book.

Keep a lookout for the boy with the sword. He is hidden in each scene...

Pyramid

The pyramids were built in ancient Egypt more than 4000 years ago. They were tombs for pharaohs, the kings of Egypt. A large pyramid took more than 20 years to complete.

Pyramids were painted a deep red. This made them stand out against the sands of the desert. Placed at the very top of the pyramid was the capstone. This was covered in gold so it would gleam in the sunlight.

Workers' village

Set square

Pharaoh

Sled

Mud and rubble

Casing stones

Teams of workers dragged huge blocks of stone on sleds up a steep ramp. The ramp, built of rubble, spiraled up the pyramid's sides.

Using wooden poles, the workers carefully levered the heavy blocks of stone off the sleds and into exactly the right position on the pyramid.

Casing stones made out of fine limestone were placed on the outside edges. This gave the pyramid a smooth outer surface.

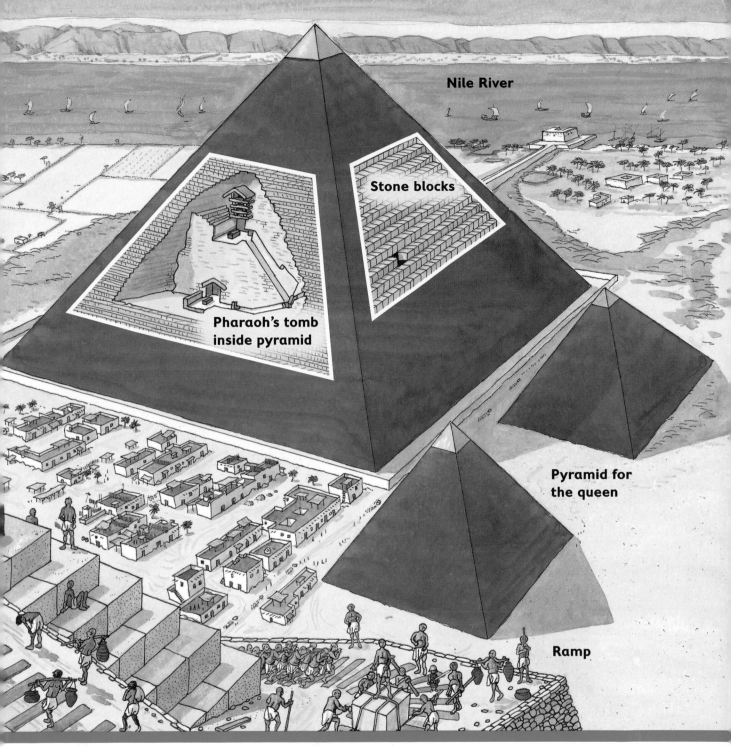

Nile River

Stone blocks

Pharaoh's tomb inside pyramid

Pyramid for the queen

Ramp

The workers used set squares to make sure all the stones were straight and level. Then they used chisels to chip away the edges so they would fit together perfectly.

The pharaoh employed a huge workforce for the job. It was made up of as many as 100,000 men. The workers received housing and food in return for their work.

The pharaoh's body would rest in a stone coffin called a sarcophagus, placed in a chamber deep inside the pyramid.

Hill Fort

Hundreds of years ago, people lived inside forts. Surrounded by a timber fence, forts were built on the tops of hills. This made them hard to attack. Outside was a ditch and a rampart, a protective ridge of dirt and rocks. Inside, round houses were built with frames made of branches and walls of mud or stone. Roofs were built from bundles of reeds, called thatch

Guard

Weaving

Cooking

Watch tower

Chariot

Warriors

Palisade (fence)

Sheep

Ramparts

Ditch

Cattle were very useful to the tribespeople. They provided them with milk, meat, and hides. Oxen were bred to pull carts carrying heavy loads.

All the boys were trained to be warriors and defend their tribe. The tribespeople were skilled metalworkers. They made metal shields and spears.

The women prepared and cooked meals over open fires inside the fort buildings. The smoke escaped through gaps in the thatch roofs.

Repairing
a thatch
roof

View inside
main building

Cattle

Chariot

Oxcart

Warriors

Pigs

Hen house

Pottery kiln

The watch tower was built over the gateway. This was the most strongly defended part of the fort. Guards could hurl spears down on attackers from behind fences.

Safe inside their hill fort, the tribespeople led simple lives. They tended their animals, grew crops, ground corn, chopped wood, and wove cloth.

Every hill fort tribe had a leader or chieftain. He led his warriors into battle against other tribes. He lived in the finest house in the fort.

Toilet block

Cells

Emperor

Gladiators

Amphitheater

Very few Roman houses had bathrooms. Instead, people went to public bath-houses to bathe, exercise, and gossip. The pools were heated by furnaces. The baths had several rooms, some with hot baths, others with cold.

Roman army commanders traveled around in chariots like this one. The Roman army conquered a vast empire. It included most of Europe, North Africa, and the Middle East.

For fun, Romans visited the amphitheater. Here they met friends and watched gladiator fights. Gladiators were slaves or prisoners who fought each other or wild animals.

Temple

Shop

Market stall

Soldiers

Inside public bath-house

Caldarium (warm bath)

Furnace

Frigidarium (cold bath)

Romans

Roman towns were busy places protected by thick walls. They had straight, grid-like streets and a large central square, called a forum. This was both a place to meet and a marketplace. People also met in baths and arenas.

Wealthy Romans lived in large houses called villas with many rooms. They could relax in the gardens or enjoy meals lying on couches. Some had private bath-rooms.

A Roman soldier was called a legionary. He wore an iron helmet and body armor over a woolen tunic. He had to carry his own sword, dagger, shield, spear, and all his food supplies.

Ordinary Roman townspeople lived in apartments. They did not have kitchens, so they bought cooked food from shops or market stalls.

11

Castle

Hundreds of years ago, powerful lords lived in castles. The high stone walls protected everyone in the castle from enemy attacks.

Castles were often built on hilltops or surrounded by water-filled moats. The main entrance to the castle was the gatehouse. This was protected by a drawbridge and a portcullis.

Battlements

Store room

Dovecote

Kitchen

Wood store

Armory

Knight's horse

In the Great Hall, the lord conducted business, received visitors, and held feasts. The lord and lady would eat from golden plates at the high table with their special guests. Less important guests sat on lower tables.

Stores of food and drink were important when the castle was under siege. The more supplies a castle had, the longer it could hold out.

Young boys had to go through years of training to become a knight. At the age of 15 they became a squire. They learned how to fight and could ride into battle with their master.

Spiral steps

Great Hall

Jesters

Guards

Battlements

Pigs

Knight

Keep

Sword practice

Cooks prepared food for the lord and his guests in the kitchen. Huge joints of meat, including wild boar or venison (deer), were cooked on a spit. The kitchen was very busy at feast times.

A knight carried a sword and a shield into battle. When taking part in a jousting tournament, he wielded a lance, which was a long pole used to topple his opponent from his horse.

The castle's spiral staircase wound upward in a clockwise direction. This gave the advantage to a swordsman defending the castle. Wielding the sword in his right hand, he could strike at an attacker standing lower on the stairs.

13

Galleon

Galleons were fast and powerful warships built about 400 years ago. They had at least three masts and tall platforms at the front (bow) and back (stern). These were armed with cannons. The Spanish used galleons to carry gold, silver, and treasure to Europe from the Americas.

Topsail ("topsul")

Crow's nest

Foresail ("forsul")

Forecastle ("fo'c'sle")

Bowsprit

Sprit sail

Gunport

Anchor

Dolphins

A lantern was fixed to the stern of the galleon on the poop deck, the highest deck on the ship. The captain slept here in the Great Cabin. His rich passengers might stroll on this deck on a long voyage. The railings of the poop deck were called gunwales.

The crow's nest was a platform fixed high up the mast. From here, a lookout kept watch for pirates. Galleons were slow and easily attacked by faster pirate ships.

The ropes and chains used to control the ship's sails were known as the rigging. Sailors used rope ladders, called ratlines, to reach the sails or climb up to the crow's nest.

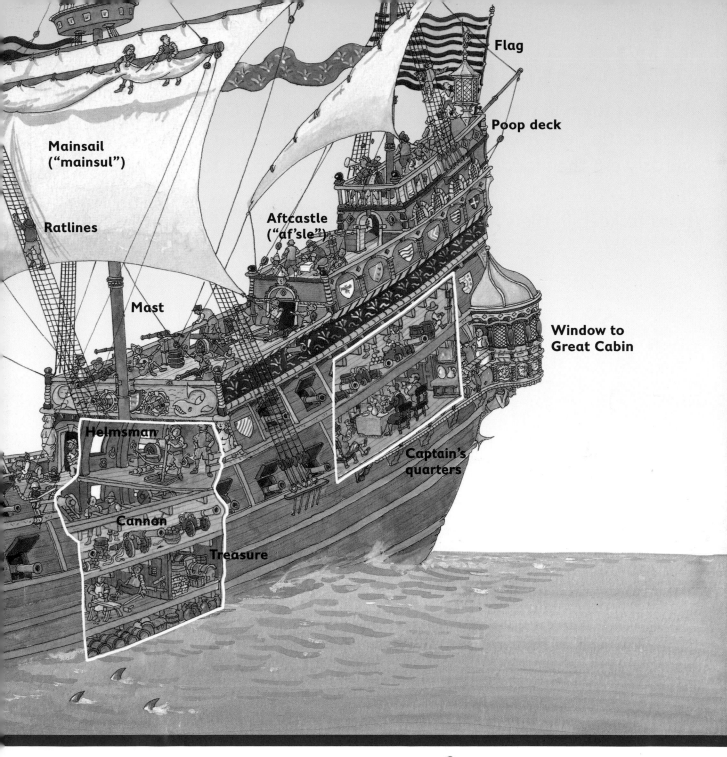

Mainsail ("mainsul")

Ratlines

Mast

Aftcastle ("af'sle")

Flag

Poop deck

Window to Great Cabin

Helmsman

Captain's quarters

Cannon

Treasure

The anchor was a large, heavy metal hook used to keep the galleon in one place in shallow water. It was fixed to the end of a long rope or chain at the ship's bow. Once lowered, it would dig into the seabed.

A galleon was armed with cannons. These were guns fixed to wheeled carriages. They could be rolled back and loaded with gunpowder and fired through gunports in the side of the ship.

The galleon's sails were attached to yards. These were poles fixed across the masts. To slow the ship down or to keep the sails from being torn apart in high winds, sailors would furl them (pull them in) using ropes called clewlines.

Wild West

This is a town in the American West in the 1870s. Cowboys drove their cattle here from ranches across the plains. Their valuable herds were then loaded onto eastbound trains to be sold in city markets. Law and order was sometimes hard to keep in the Wild West!

STORE

Jail

HOTEL

Wagon

Stage-coach

Trough

Shoot-out

Cattle

Cowboys would visit the local saloon for a drink. Trouble often followed. Fights would break out and cowboys were always ready to reach for their guns. The sheriff would try and restore order.

A sheriff was a law officer, like a policeman, appointed by a county. He made sure that the townspeople did not break any rules. He also dealt with crimes such as fights and thefts.

Townspeople shopped for basic supplies at the dry goods store. Tools and medicine, among other things, were sold here. Fresh meat was available at the butcher's shop.

16

Church

Windmill

Train

P. & L. R.R.

BANK

Saloon

Hold-up

...e were driven into town
...wboys on horseback.
...were valuable livestock
...argeted by robbers
...n as cattle rustlers.

Stagecoaches traveled the dusty roads of the American West. They took people across the plains and from town to town. Passengers were always at risk from an ambush by outlaws.

Remote towns in the Wild West often attracted outlaws, too. Outlaws led a life of crime, not only stealing cattle and robbing travelers, but also holding up banks or trains for valuables.

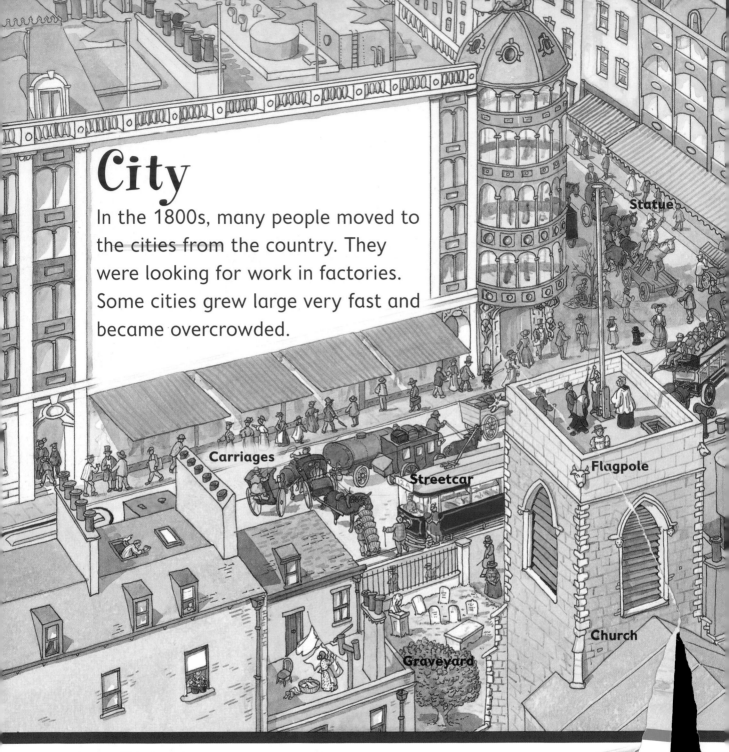

City

In the 1800s, many people moved to the cities from the country. They were looking for work in factories. Some cities grew large very fast and became overcrowded.

Statue

Carriages

Streetcar

Flagpole

Church

Graveyard

Sewage and water pipes ran beneath city streets. These helped to make cities cleaner places—they were far better than open drains.

Trams are buses that run on rails laid into the road. Electric trams replaced horse-drawn ones. Overhead electricity cables provide the power.

The narrow, cobbled 19th-century city we with people. The poo cramped, decaying h known as slums, whil people lived in fine ho

Cattle by cov They often nown

Museum

Department store

Wealthy townhouse

Apartments

Tram

Sewage pipes

Wealthy people employed servants to clean and cook for them. Their children would be cared for by nannies. Their houses had bathrooms, a luxury in those days.

Most of the vehicles in town were drawn by horses. Heavy carts were used to transport goods, such as barrels of beer. People traveled by carriages or by hansom cab.

Wealthy people visited department stores to buy expensive clothes. These large shops sold a wide range of goods, such as furniture and toys, all under one roof.

Lifeboats

First class cabins

Boiler Room

Rich passengers traveled first class. They had luxurious rooms with lots of space. Poorer passenges were not allowed here. They slept on the lower decks.

The lookout spotted the iceberg just before midnight, but it was too late. The iceberg struck *Titanic*. Her hull was badly damaged and the ship rapidly began to flood.

Titanic carried 20 lifeboats. Women and children were the first passengers allowed into the lifeboats. Some people did not believe that they were in danger and refused to get in.

Titanic

On April 10th, 1912, *Titanic* set sail across the Atlantic Ocean. It was the first voyage of the most luxurious ship ever built. *Titanic* had over 2000 passengers on board. But disaster struck one night...

She hit an iceberg, which cut a hole in her side. The ship began to fill with water. The crew helped passengers into lifeboats, but there weren't enough boats to save everyone. *Titanic* sunk with 1500 people still on board. Many perished in the icy waters.

Crane

Cabins

Cargo

The cargo was stored in the lower part of the ship's hull. It weighed 1400 tons. These areas of the ship were the first to flood. The crew were sleeping on the lower decks. They tried to escape to the upper decks but the water was coming up fast...

The boiler rooms were also deep in the hull of the ship. They flooded soon after *Titanic* struck the iceberg. The crew had to keep the pumps and lighting going

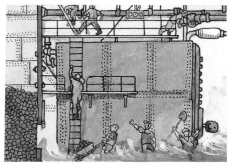

for as long as possible. When the order came to abandon ship, it was too late for many of the crew to climb out and escape.

Index

Did you find him?

pages 6-7

pages 8-9

pages 10-11

pages 12-13

pages 14-15

pages 16-17

pages 18-19

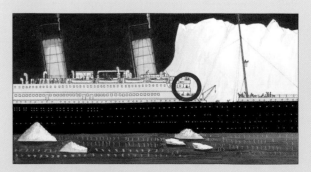

pages 20-21

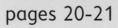

For more great fiction and nonfiction, go to www.windmillbooks.com